J621.873 Mur
Murray, J.
Cranes.
Caledon Public Library
FEB 2019   3582

PRICE: $20.15 (3582/02   )

D1281436

Construction Machines

Cranes

Dash!
LEVELED READERS
An Imprint of Abdo Zoom • abdobooks.com

2

Dash!
LEVELED READERS

Level 1 – Beginning
Short and simple sentences with familiar words or patterns for children who are beginning to understand how letters and sounds go together.

Level 2 – Emerging
Longer words and sentences with more complex language patterns for readers who are practicing common words and letter sounds.

Level 3 – Transitional
More developed language and vocabulary for readers who are becoming more independent.

abdobooks.com

Published by Abdo Zoom, a division of ABDO, PO Box 398166, Minneapolis, Minnesota 55439.
Copyright © 2019 by Abdo Consulting Group, Inc. International copyrights reserved in all countries.
No part of this book may be reproduced in any form without written permission from the publisher.
Dash!™ is a trademark and logo of Abdo Zoom.

Printed in the United States of America, North Mankato, Minnesota.
092018
012019

Photo Credits: AP Images, Getty Images, iStock, Shutterstock
Production Contributors: Kenny Abdo, Jennie Forsberg, Grace Hansen, John Hansen
Design Contributors: Dorothy Toth, Neil Klinepier

Library of Congress Control Number: 2018945600

Publisher's Cataloging in Publication Data

Names: Murray, Julie, author.
Title: Cranes / by Julie Murray.
Description: Minneapolis, Minnesota : Abdo Zoom, 2019 | Series: Construction
      machines | Includes online resources and index.
Identifiers: ISBN 9781532125157 (lib. bdg.) | ISBN 9781641856607 (pbk.) |
      ISBN 9781532126178 (ebook) | ISBN 9781532126680 (Read-to-me ebook)
Subjects: LCSH: Cranes, derricks, etc--Juvenile literature. | Construction
      equipment--Juvenile literature. | Machinery--Construction--Juvenile literature.
Classification: DDC 621.8--dc23

THIS BOOK CONTAINS
RECYCLED MATERIALS

Table of Contents

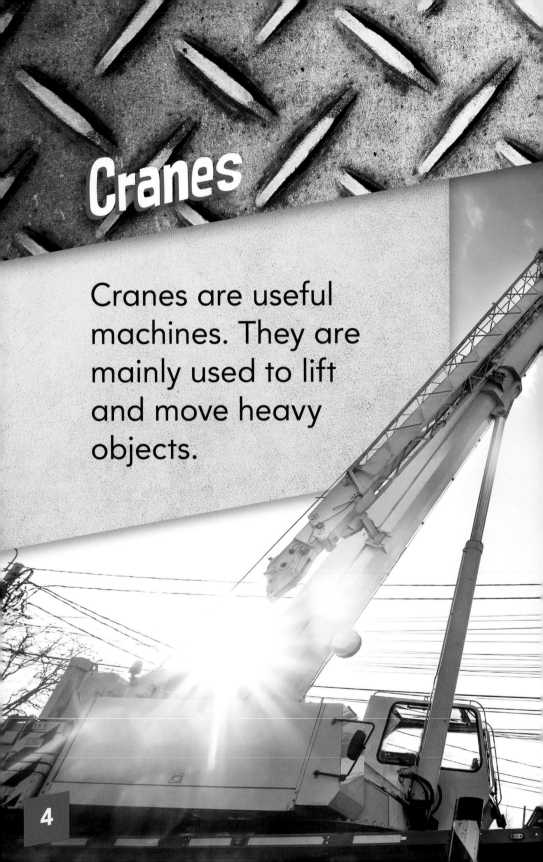

Cranes

Cranes are useful machines. They are mainly used to lift and move heavy objects.

Cranes are used at construction sites where they move giant beams.

A crane has many parts. It has a cab and a **boom**. It also has a **pulley**, a cable, and a hook.

The operator controls the **boom**. The **pulley** allows the cable to move up and down. The hook holds the **load**.

A wrecking ball can be added to the hook. It swings back and forth. It knocks down buildings!

Kinds of Cranes

There are many kinds of cranes. Mobile cranes have wheels. They can drive from one job to another.

Crawler cranes are on tracks. They move safely over loose ground.

Tower cranes are tall. They are used for jobs that are up high. The long arm is called a jib.

A floating crane is used in water. It can help **load** things on and off ships.

More Facts

- Cranes are named after a bird. People thought they looked like the long-necked crane.

- The Ancient Greeks were the first to use cranes. Then, cranes were powered by men and animals.

- The Asian Hercules III is one of the most powerful cranes. It can lift 5,000 tons (4,535.9 metric tons)!

Glossary

boom – the long arm that moves left and right and connects the arm and bucket to the main body of the machine.

load – the amount of something carried.

pulley – a machine made from a wheel or set of wheels with grooves that a rope or chain can be pulled over. It helps lift things.

Index

load 11

operator 11

parts 8, 11, 13, 18

terrain 16

tracks 16

types 14, 16, 18, 20

uses 4, 7, 14, 18

water 20

wheels 14

Online Resources

Booklinks
NONFICTION NETWORK
FREE! ONLINE NONFICTION RESOURCES

To learn more about cranes, please visit **abdobooklinks.com**. These links are routinely monitored and updated to provide the most current information available.